Psycho

OSCAR ICHAZO

ARICA INSTITUTE

SIMON AND SCHUSTER • NEW YORK

calisthenics

Copyright © 1976 by Arica Institute, Inc.
All rights reserved
including the right of reproduction
in whole or in part in any form
Published by Simon and Schuster
A Gulf+Western Company
Rockefeller Center, 630 Fifth Avenue
New York, New York 10020
Manufactured in the United States of America
1 2 3 4 5 6 7 8 9 10

Arica and ⬡ are registered service marks of Arica Institute, Inc.
Psychocalisthenics is a service mark of Arica Institute, Inc.

Library of Congress Cataloging in Publication Data

Arica Institute.
  Psychocalisthenics.

    1. Exercise. 2. Mind and body. 3. Mental
hygiene. I. Title. [DNLM: 1. Gymnastics.
QT255 A697p]
RA781.A74   1976   613.7   76-118
ISBN 0-671-22237-6
ISBN 0-671-22238-4 pbk.

Photographs by Peter Schlessinger

CONTENTS

**PART TWO: ADVANCED STAGES OF
PSYCHOCALISTHENICS**

**PART THREE: PSYCHOCALISTHENICS EXERCISES
FOR SPECIAL PURPOSES**

CONTENTS

**PART TWO: ADVANCED STAGES OF
PSYCHOCALISTHENICS**

**PART THREE: PSYCHOCALISTHENICS EXERCISES
FOR SPECIAL PURPOSES**

INTRODUCTION

Psychocalisthenics is a sequence of exercises designed to restore the balance of the body and the psyche. *Psychocalisthenics* integrates mind, emotions and body, which must function together if we are to attain our best possible condition as human beings. This sequence of exercises moves the entire body as economically as possible, under the control of the breath. This is what makes *psychocalisthenics* different from other exercises. In calisthenics the movement is done by muscles. In *psychocalisthenics* the movement is controlled by the breath.

Psychocalisthenics puts three fundamental aspects of a human being—mind, emotions, body—in tune with one another. When we work with these three aspects, we make the exercises stronger, since each aspect supports the others. And when we have a triangle of mind, body and emotions working together in unity, we obtain a complete experience of our being.

An imbalance occurs in our lives because our body and our psyche work in constant opposition to each other. The physical body has its own limitations; it is subject to rules for the maintenance of health and to all the physical laws which govern its development. These physical laws impose restrictions on the psyche, which develops independently of the body. The aims and aspirations of the psyche oppose those of the body. In the normal life of a human being a permanent contradiction exists between the ambitions of the psyche and the limitations of the body.

Suppose we wish to undertake some physical task that demands strength in excess of our body's capacity. Our psychic purpose may be so strong that we overpower our body. Our body responds by becoming sick. In time this sickness affects our psyche by making it ill as well. In this contest neither side wins. Only by balancing body and mind, so that their aims and aspirations are in harmony rather than in contradiction, can we have a complete life.

Consciousness is life itself. Consciousness, life, in a human being is body and mind. In animals there is no such separation. In animals all consciousness functions through the body and expresses itself through the body. There is no mind expression at all. For animals the body is everything. For human beings it is not. In the scale of evolution, only human beings have developed a mind distinct from their body.

In *psychocalisthenics* we work to refine our body. This refinement will also be experienced in our mind. The more refined our body, the clearer our mind.

Mind has pain, just as the body has pain. When the body is in pain, consciousness goes to the body. When the mind is in pain, consciousness goes to the mind. Pain for the mind is preoccupations, anxiety, and fear. Animals have no fear in this sense. The action of saving themselves is complete. In human beings, it is not. Stress can paralyze a human being totally, because he immediately falls into the conflict of body and mind. The body wants escape; the mind does not know what to do. The result is paralysis. This conflict between mind and body produces most illness in human beings.

Muscular tension results from the permanent internal conflict between body and mind. Tension also results from the fight between human beings and their environment. Another cause of tension is the internal conflict between a human being's idea of what he should be doing and what he *is* doing right at this moment. Mind is a social development. Human beings fight their society all the time. Our normal experience in technological society causes tension and stress. To eliminate tension, we use *psychocalisthenics.*

The link between body and mind is breath. Breathing connects us with our environment. Through breathing, we feel our environment physically and psychically. The amount of energy available for the functioning of our brain and all the rest of our body is directly proportionate to the amount of air in our lungs, which determines the amount of oxygen available to our cells.

The link of the breath is expressed as our emotional condition. If our blood is too acid, the result is depression or bad humor. Conversely, if our blood is too alkaline, the result is overenthusiasm that causes us to burn more energy than is necessary. Very soon this overenthusiasm is followed by depression. Both states are an imbalance in our emotions. They also indicate an imbalance, a weakness, in our body. A body that is easily strained by emotion or one that does not react emotionally is weak.

We can recover our emotional balance by regulating the acid-base equilibrium of the blood with breathing exercises. When this balance is achieved, our body and our mind begin working together in unity. The psyche is the expression of the body at the same time that the body is the expression of the psyche. The breathing patterns in *psychocalisthenics* make the link between mind and body.

Several different conditions are necessary for the health of a human body. It has to be a resistant body. It has to be a flexible body. It has to be an economical body, in the sense that it can function with the minimum amount of effort rather than the maximum. Finally it has to be a body that coordinates the total psyche of a human being.

There are two distinct groups of muscles that make two types of body movements. The large muscles, the muscles of strength, reach for things; the little muscles repel things. A balanced combination of these two muscle groups gives flexibility. If one group of muscles dominates the other, the body is weak and inelastic. Elasticity is the midpoint between a body that is musclebound and one that has atrophied due to insufficient exercise. *Psychocalisthenics* increases flexibility by exercising and balancing both muscle groups.

Psychocalisthenics includes all the movements necessary for a complete kinesthetic expression of our body. To feel kinesthetically is to have the impression of our body in movement, that is, to be aware of the kinesthetic relation of all our bones and muscles. When we move fast, we lose kinesthetic awareness. When we move all our body kinesthetically, we produce a complete movement of our psyche. Thus our kinesthetic sensibility makes another link that unifies mind, body, and emotions. In *psychocalisthenics* we use slow motion to make us aware of our kinesthetic sense. Then we are conscious of the movement of our body. We are aware of the movement itself rather than the outcome of the movement.

Arica has developed *psychocalisthenics* as a complete exercise for human beings. The human body is the result of the entire scale of our planetary evolution. It is a result in the same specific way that the fruit of the tree is the result of the entire process of the tree. Thus we do not see evolution in the Darwinian way, as conflict between species, but as a process of development. This process follows a pre-established plan of evolution; this plan of evolution ends with human beings. So we understand the human body as the final result, the completion of one entire process. In the body of a human being evolution is completed.

OSCAR ICHAZO

GENERAL RECOMMENDATIONS

Practice *psychocalisthenics* regularly to develop relaxation, endurance, emotional stability, flexibility, and resistance to stress.

To practice *psychocalisthenics* you will need:
- a room with good ventilation
- loose-fitting clothes
- a mat or rug
- an area of clear floor space approximately 6 feet by 6 feet

Begin by studying *Part One,* The Exercises. Follow the *learning sequence* provided in *stage one*—Learning the Movements. This learning sequence is the same for all stages. Having completed *stage one* in the first month, go on to *stage two*—Muscular Conditioning. Practice each stage for approximately one month.

Once you have learned *psychocalisthenics,* do the entire sequence in order, allowing half an hour a day, Monday through Friday. The optimum time for doing *psychocalisthenics* is fifteen minutes after waking up.

Psychocalisthenics may be accompanied by music if done as physical exercise. If done as meditation, silence is preferable.

Over a period of years several thousand people have practiced and tested *psychocalisthenics. Psychocalisthenics* exercises the entire body. Doing too much too quickly may result in soreness and strain. People of any age may do these exercises. Older people should use moderation, spending longer in *stage one.* If you have any doubts about your physical ability to do *psychocalisthenics,* see your doctor, especially if you have a history of back or heart problems.

Concentration, a positive attitude, a relaxed approach to the exercises, and enthusiasm are all indispensable for achieving good results with *psychocalisthenics.*

Throughout *psychocalisthenics,* place your concentration in a point located about four finger-widths below your navel, called the *kath point.*

Inhale through your nose and exhale through your mouth throughout *psychocalisthenics.* Fill your lungs from the bottom to the top, letting your breath move your body. The drawings indicate breathing patterns: black arrows mean inhalation; white arrows mean exhalation.

Psychocalisthenics is learned in five stages. Each stage prepares you for the next. It takes about a month to complete each stage. In *stage one* you learn the exercises in sequence. In *stage two* you condition your muscles and develop stamina and stronger breathing. In *stage three* you condition your emotions by concentrating on your breathing. In *stage four* you develop awareness of your kinesthetic sensibility. And in *stage five, psychocalisthenics* becomes a complete meditation in movement and color.

FOOT POSITIONS

Before you start learning the exercises, become familiar with the foot positions. For each exercise there is a breathing pattern and a foot position which assure the greatest benefit.

The distance between the feet is measured in foot-widths. Be as accurate as possible. Having the feet parallel means that the second toes point straight ahead. This may feel pigeon-toed at first.

It is easier to plant yourself firmly on the ground if you do the exercises barefoot.

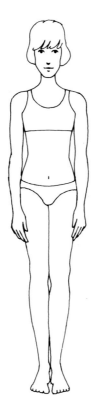

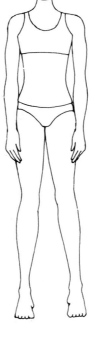

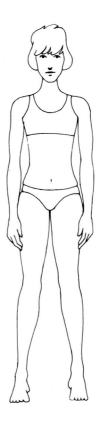

Position of equilibrium
Feet flush against each other.

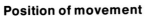

Position of movement
Feet parallel, 1½ foot-widths apart.

Standing position
Feet parallel, 2 foot-widths apart.

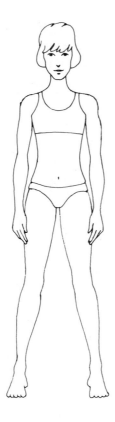

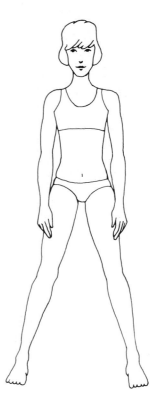

Position of strength

Feet parallel, 3 foot-widths apart. This is approximately shoulder-width.

Position of relaxation

Feet parallel, 5 foot-widths apart. This is the farthest apart the feet can be placed without breaking the keystone of the arch formed by the legs and pelvis.

part one

The First Stage
of Psychocalisthenics

STAGE ONE | LEARNING THE MOVEMENTS

The first stage of *psychocalisthenics* is for committing the exercises and the sequence of the exercises to memory. Learning the exercise means being able to do the exercise exactly as described in the procedure. Learning these exercises and doing them regularly helps you focus your energy.

The exercises are simple and they work the whole body. However, do not do too much too quickly. Respect the limits of your body. Begin *psychocalisthenics* on a Monday. Allow half an hour a day, Monday through Friday. In this stage, do the movements at a medium tempo.

LEARNING SEQUENCE

For each exercise, read the procedure several times, then do the exercise as precisely as possible. The following schedule is recommended:

WEEK 1

Monday: Following the exercise procedure, do each exercise listed below.

1. *Integration breath*
2. *Headstand*
3. *Picking grapes*
4. *Lateral stretch*
5. *Flamingo*
6. *Ax 1 and 2*
7. *Udiyama*
8. *Shoulder rolls*

Tuesday: Practice the exercises learned on Monday. Then practice the following new exercises.

9. *Arm circles*
10. *Hand circles*
11. *Windmill*
12. *Scythe*

Wednesday: Practice the exercises learned on Monday and Tuesday. Then practice the following new exercises.

13. *Neck series*
    Head rolls
    Side-to-side
    Camel
    Lung breath
14. *Candle (2 minutes)*
15. *Belly series*
    Bow

Thursday: Practice the exercises learned previously. Then practice the following new exercises.

15. *Belly series*
     Leg circles
     Leg scissors
16. *Zero position*
17. *Cobra*

Friday: Practice all the exercises learned so far. Then practice the following new exercises.

18. *Pendulum*
19. *Completo*

WEEK 2

Practice the entire sequence, half an hour a day, Monday through Friday. Remember the *integration breath* between exercises where indicated. Refer to the procedure for each exercise, even if you think you already know it. If you finish the sequence in less than 30 minutes, adjust your timing the next day.

On Friday, try to do all the exercises from memory; check the procedure to see if you did each movement accurately and maintained the correct breathing pattern and foot position.

WEEK 3

Continue practicing the entire sequence half an hour a day, Monday through Friday, from memory. Now begin studying the introduction to each exercise and the hints that follow.

Concentrate on making the movements smooth and rhythmical. Be aware of the different areas of the body being worked by each exercise.

WEEK 4

Practice the entire sequence half an hour a day, Monday through Friday, from memory. Now you should know every aspect of *psychocalisthenics:* movements, breathing patterns, foot positions, areas of the body and hints.

THE EXERCISES

INTEGRATION BREATH 3x

Integration breath is the first exercise of *psychocalisthenics.*

With *integration breath* we remember that our breath is doing the movement. Do the *integration breath* in slow motion, keeping in mind that the breath is moving the arms.

The physical effect of this exercise is to restore the normal activity of the body after the effort of the previous exercise. The *integration breath* rebalances and reconditions our entire system.

The psychological effect of *integration breath* is calming because it returns equilibrium to our body. As our lungs breathe fully and consciously our entire body begins to feel the well-being of that breathing, and this produces a feeling of rest and peace.

Procedure

Standing position

1. Stand with your feet parallel, 2 foot-widths apart.

Your shoulders are relaxed, arms hanging at your sides.

Knees are slightly bent.

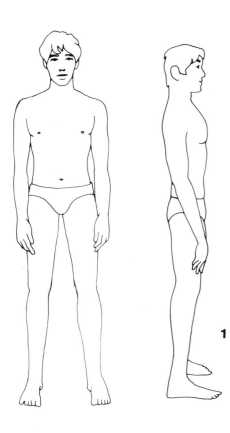

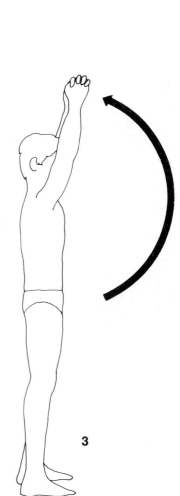

2. Let your arms hang in front of your body.

Join your hands, fingers loosely interlaced.

3. Inhaling slowly and evenly, raise your arms slowly up and over your head.

The movement comes from the shoulders; the arms are extended and relaxed.

The breath should command the movement of the arms. Feel that your breath is lifting your arms.

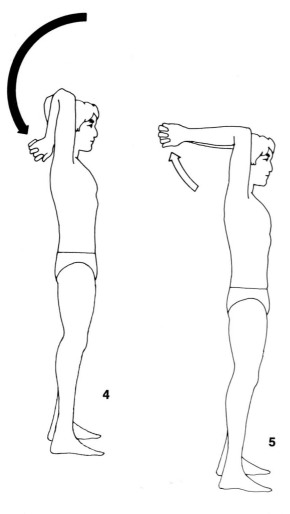

4. Still inhaling, let the forearms and hands drop down behind your neck. Press the heels of your hands together.

5. Exhaling evenly, slowly bring your hands and forearms over your head.

Imagine that your arms float down on a cushion of air.

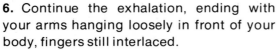

6. Continue the exhalation, ending with your arms hanging loosely in front of your body, fingers still interlaced.

Your arms remain extended throughout the movement.

Do the exercise 3 times.

Hints

Always do the *integration breath* in slow motion.

When doing the *integration breath* between exercises, be sure to check your feet: they should be 2 foot-widths apart and parallel.

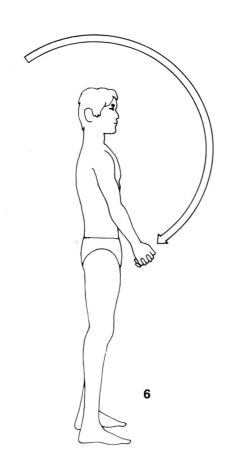

HEADSTAND 1x

The *headstand* is an exercise from Hatha Yoga.

The natural position of the human body is a head up, feet down position. When you reverse this polarity, the body experiences a slight stress. Physically, the pressure of the blood in the brain increases. The additional blood in the cortex produces relaxation in the brain.

Psychologically, the effect is lightness. When you stand up again, your body feels lighter and your brain feels rested.

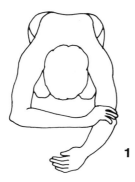

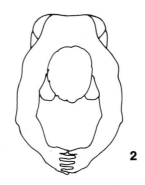

Procedure

1. Kneel on the floor and place your elbows a forearm's length apart.

Breathe normally.

2. Interlace your fingers so that an equilateral triangle is formed by the two elbows and the hands.

This triangle is vital for a stable *headstand*.

3. Place the top of your head flat on the floor resting against your hands.

Your hands will serve as a brace for your head.

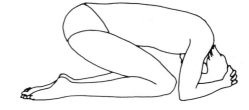

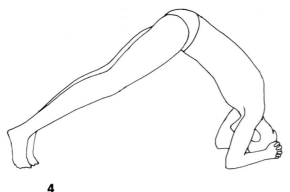

4

4. Beginning from the kneeling position, straighten your legs, feet on tiptoe.

5. Walk forward on your toes toward your head. The buttocks will come up naturally.

Check that your elbows and hands still form an equilateral triangle.

5

6. Slowly begin lifting your feet off the floor.

Tuck your knees against your chest and balance yourself before straightening your legs to a vertical position.

Keep most of the weight on your forearms rather than your head.

6

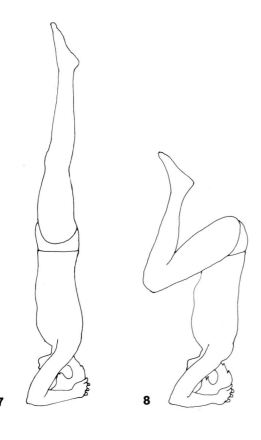

7. Straighten your legs to a vertical position. Hold the vertical position with your toes pointing up for 1 to 3 minutes.

8. To come down, bend your knees slowly and return to the tucked position.

Lower your legs, touch your toes to the floor, then come down into the kneeling position.

9. The buttocks rest on the heels, forehead on the floor.

Rest in this position for 1 to 2 minutes before standing.

Stand up and do 1 *integration breath.*

Hints

If you feel that a free-standing *headstand* is too difficult at first, use a wall for support. Begin by kneeling so that your interlaced hands are a palm's length from the wall. As your sense of balance gradually improves, you will know when to try the *headstand* unsupported. Approach the *headstand* cautiously.

Do the *headstand* on a rug with enough open space around you to keep you from bumping into any furniture in case you should fall. If you should fall, fall relaxed.

PICKING GRAPES 6x

Picking grapes is an exercise of contraction and extension of the entire skeletal system. Exhaling with the contraction, followed by inhaling with the extension, accelerates the metabolism. More oxygen is demanded by the muscles and taken in by the full inhalation. Circulation increases to keep pace. The physical effect is an increase in available energy.

Psychologically, too, you are energized, becoming more alert and more aware of your body.

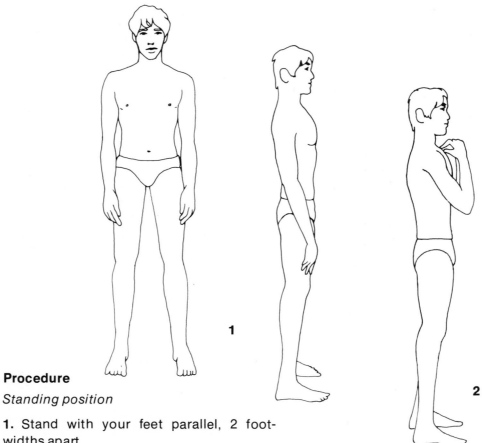

Procedure

Standing position

1. Stand with your feet parallel, 2 foot-widths apart.

Your shoulders are relaxed, arms hanging at your sides.

Knees are slightly bent.

2. With your arms and shoulders relaxed, elbows at your sides, touch your fingers lightly to your shoulders.

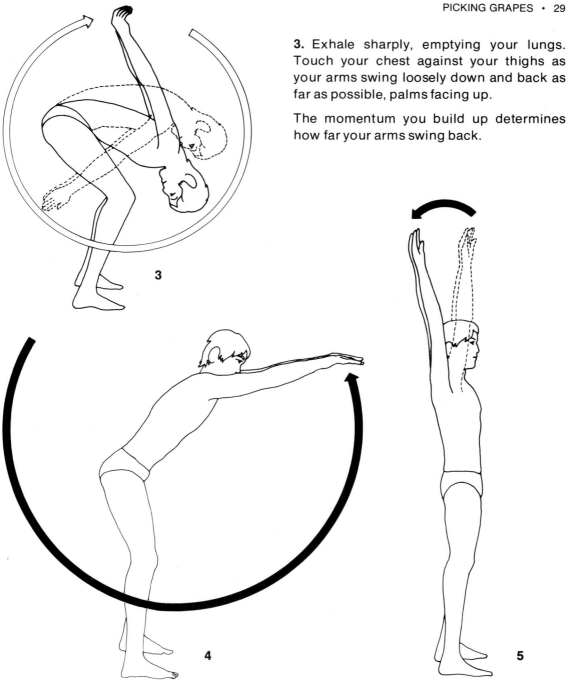

3. Exhale sharply, emptying your lungs. Touch your chest against your thighs as your arms swing loosely down and back as far as possible, palms facing up.

The momentum you build up determines how far your arms swing back.

4. Inhaling, raise your arms above your head with a swinging motion that straightens your body.

In the most extended position the palms face forward.

5. Pump your arms and shoulders back and forth 4 times, inhaling sharply with each backward movement.

The momentum you build up determines how far back you can pump your arms.

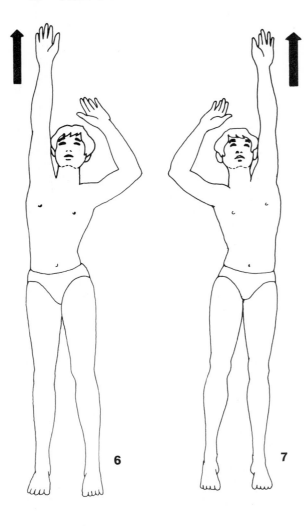

6. With arms still extended over your head, look up and inhale sharply as you reach up with your right hand.

The left heel lifts slightly as you reach with the right hand.

The idea is that you are reaching for a bunch of grapes that is out of reach.

7. Inhaling sharply, looking upward, reach as high as possible with the left hand, lifting the right heel slightly as you reach.

Reach up again with the right hand and then with the left, inhaling sharply each time.

Return your fingers to your shoulders, and you are ready to begin again.

Do the exercise 6 times
Do 1 *integration breath.*

Hints

Breathe deeply, so that the air seems to travel right down into your *kath point* (see page 12) on the inhalation. This will improve your sense of balance as well as your breathing.

Let the movements become a dance, once you know them by heart. Do them gracefully, rhythmically, lightly.

LATERAL STRETCH 6x

Lateral stretch works with the muscles of the back, chest and belly. Emotional tension expresses itself as tense muscles in these areas.

In the psyche, emotional tension is expressed as fear of losing equilibrium. When we challenge this fear by stretching to the limit of physical equilibrium, physical and emotional tensions are relaxed.

Procedure

Position of strength

1. Stand with your feet parallel, 3 foot-widths apart.

Your shoulders are relaxed, arms hanging at your sides.

Knees are unlocked.

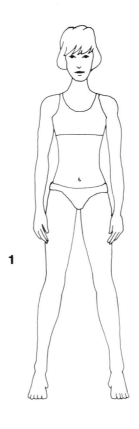

2. Raise your arms straight over your head and parallel to each other.

The palms face each other.

3. Inhaling, bend your body as far as possible to the left, arms as straight as possible, palms facing each other.

Resist the tendency to bend either forward or backward as you lean to the side. Your head faces forward.

Let the weight of the right arm stretch the muscles along the right side.

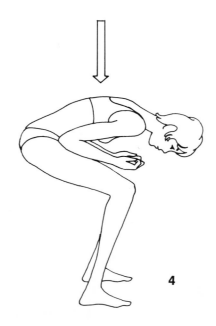

4. Sharply exhale all the air as your elbows snap to the sides of your body, hands closing to form loose fists.

The elbows are tucked in alongside the rib cage, not poking into the belly.

At the same time, your knees bend and the torso leans forward from the hips.

5. Inhaling, come up from the tucked position and simultaneously bend your body as far as possible to the right, arms straight, palms facing each other.

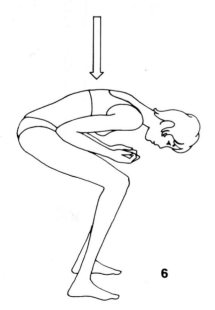

6. Exhaling sharply, return to the tucked position and continue the exercise.

Do the exercise 6 times.
Do 1 *integration breath*.

Hints

Feel as though the exhalation is dropping you, the inhalation picking you up.

When coming up from the tucked position, bend your body to the side as you come up. Do not straighten up first and then bend to the side.

FLAMINGO 6x

The *flamingo* is an exercise in letting go of our emotions. Holding on to our emotions produces tension. The movement of the *flamingo* is a controlled fall, as in diving, so that we lose fear of letting go.

Physically, the muscles of the lower back, pelvis and belly are loosened and stretched.

Psychologically, we release emotional tension.

Procedure

Position of movement

1. Stand with your feet parallel, 1½ foot-widths apart.

Your shoulders are relaxed, arms hanging at your sides.

Knees are unlocked.

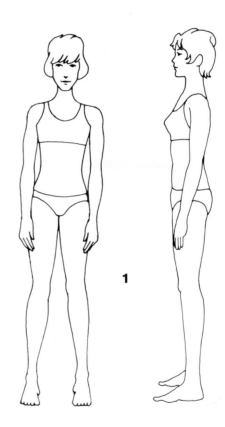

1

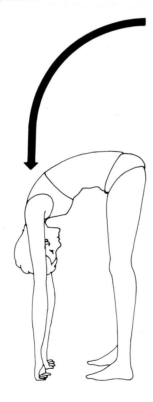

2

2. Inhaling, let your body fall forward bending from the base of the spine, keeping the knees straight. The arms and head are relaxed and hang down in front of the body. This stretches the muscles of the lower back.

Your knuckles touch the floor 12 inches in front of your toes. Most of the weight is on the toes. The heels remain on the floor.

If the muscles and tendons of your legs are too tight to let you reach the floor, bend over only as far as you can without bending your knees.

Hold the position for a moment, keeping the legs straight so as to create a stretch in the calves.

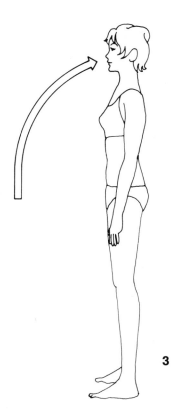

3. Exhaling, return to an upright position, keeping your back straight.

Hold this position briefly before repeating the exercise.

Do the exercise 6 times.
Do 1 *integration breath.*

3

AX 1   6x

The movements of *ax 1* serve two purposes. They stretch all the muscle groups that rotate the trunk around the pelvis. These muscles sustain the equilibrium of the spinal column. *Ax 1* also produces a snakelike movement of the entire length of the spinal column which massages each vertebra. This massage invigorates the entire nervous system by relaxing tensions around the rachidial nerves, the large nerves which radiate from the spine.

Psychologically, this exercise has the effect of further integrating mind and body.

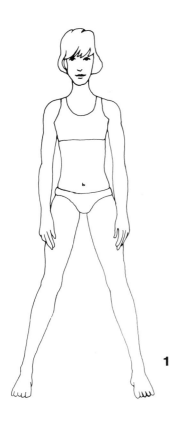

1

Procedure

Position of relaxation

1. Stand with your feet parallel, 5 foot-widths apart.

Your shoulders are relaxed, arms hanging at your sides.

Knees are slightly bent.

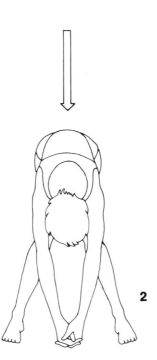

2

3

2. Bend forward and let your arms hang in front of your body as close to the floor as possible.

Interlace your fingers.

3. Inhaling, rotate the torso in a half-circle up and to the left, allowing your arms to swing up and over your head as you come to a standing position. Your arms remain extended.

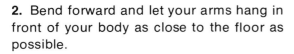

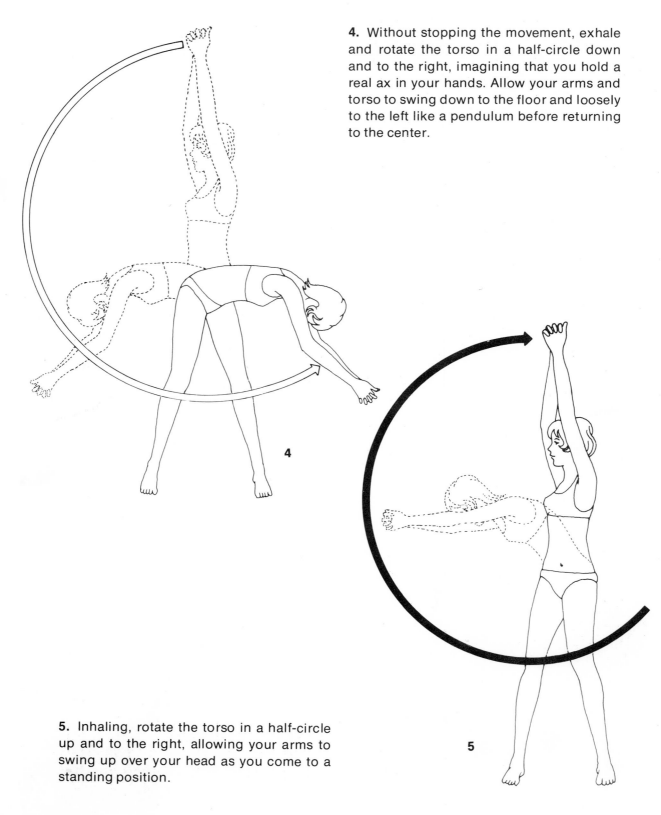

4. Without stopping the movement, exhale and rotate the torso in a half-circle down and to the right, imagining that you hold a real ax in your hands. Allow your arms and torso to swing down to the floor and loosely to the left like a pendulum before returning to the center.

5. Inhaling, rotate the torso in a half-circle up and to the right, allowing your arms to swing up over your head as you come to a standing position.

6. Without stopping the movement, exhale and rotate the torso in a half-circle down and to the left, allowing your arms and torso to swing down to the floor and loosely to the right like a pendulum before returning to the center.

From this position you are ready to begin again.

Do the exercise 6 times.
Go on to *ax 2* without doing an *integration breath*.

Hints

The circular movement of *ax 1* is continuous. Be sure to keep the knees and hips loose, and the arms extended. As you become accustomed to the body movement, you will notice that the torso rotates naturally during this exercise. Become aware of the undulating, snakelike movement of your spine.

Let the weight of your body make the greatest possible stretch in each rotation.

6

AX 2 3x

The movements of *ax 2* serve two purposes. They stretch all the muscle groups that rotate the trunk around the pelvis. These muscles sustain the equilibrium of the spinal column.

Ax 2 also produces a snakelike movement of the entire length of the spinal column which massages each vertebra. This massage invigorates the entire nervous system by relaxing tensions around the rachidial nerves, the large nerves which radiate from the spine.

Psychologically, this exercise has the effect of further integrating mind and body.

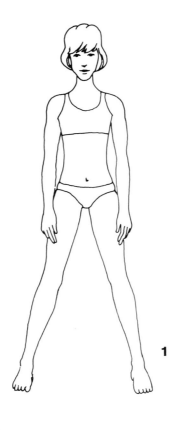

Procedure

Position of relaxation

1. Stand with your feet parallel, 5 footwidths apart.

Your shoulders are relaxed, arms hanging at your sides.

Knees are slightly bent.

2. Interlace your fingers and lift your arms as far above your head as possible.

In this position, exhale sharply, emptying your lungs.

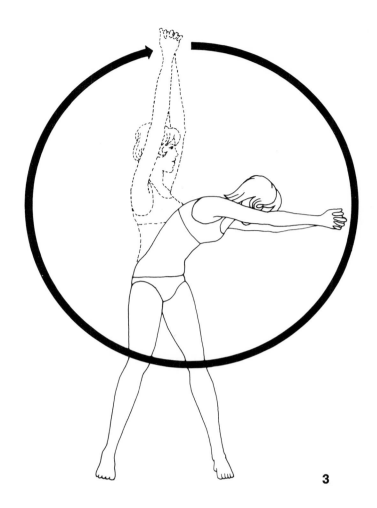

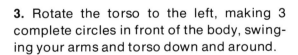

3

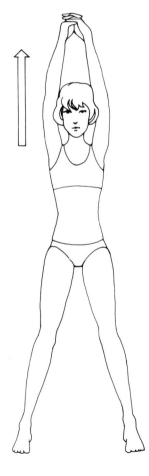

3. Rotate the torso to the left, making 3 complete circles in front of the body, swinging your arms and torso down and around.

Gauge your lung capacity so that you inhale evenly throughout the 3 circles, ending with your lungs full.

The 3 circles are one continuous movement.

End the set of 3 circles with your arms above your head, and exhale sharply, emptying your lungs.

4. Inhaling evenly throughout the 3 circles, repeat the movement 3 times to the right.

End the set of 3 circles with your arms above your head, and exhale sharply, emptying your lungs.

From this position you are ready to begin again to the left.

Do the exercise 3 times.
Do 1 *integration breath.*

Hints

Even more clearly than in the single circle of *ax 1,* feel here that the circular motion involves torso, hips and spine as one flexible unit. Feel your arms flung into orbit by the movement of your lower spine.

UDIYAMA   3x

Udiyama is a Hatha Yoga exercise.

The colon, at the end of the alimentary canal, can be seen as the final part of our organism. It receives the end products of the pressure of our daily lives. *Udiyama* is an exercise that flexes the colon.

Physically, *udiyama* cleanses the body by massaging the colon.

Psychologically, *udiyama* leaves you feeling at ease with yourself.

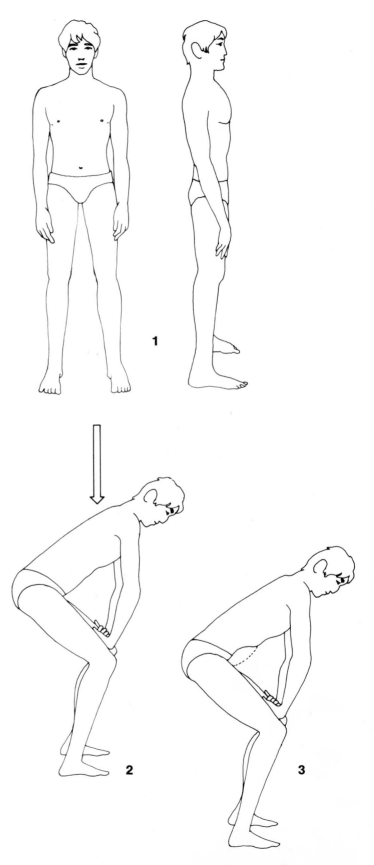

Procedure

Position of strength

1. Stand with your feet parallel, 3 foot-widths apart.

Your shoulders are relaxed, arms hanging at your sides.

2. Bend your knees and place your hands on your thighs just above the knees with your fingers pointing inward. Your shoulders, arms and hands are relaxed. Your spine and neck are straight. Check the buttock muscles; they should remain relaxed.

Exhale sharply, emptying your lungs and forcing the stomach out.

3. Keeping the lungs empty, alternately contract and relax the abdominal muscles in rapid succession 20 times. Make each contraction as deep as possible.

Keep the movements of the belly smooth and regular.

A pull in the throat occurs each time the belly is pumped.

Do the exercise 3 times.
Do 1 *integration breath*.

Hints

Keep your head and spine in a straight line.

SHOULDER ROLLS   6x

Shoulder rolls is a mechanical exercise that works the muscle groups of the shoulders as well as the muscle groups that control breathing and respiration. *Shoulder rolls* also enlarges the thorax, increasing our ability to breathe, and this contributes to our emotional balance. This balance depends precisely on how good the quality of our breathing is.

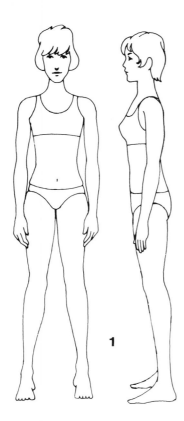

Procedure

Standing position

1. Stand with your feet parallel, 2 foot-widths apart.

Your shoulders are relaxed, arms hanging at your sides.

Knees are unlocked.

2. The right hand clasps the left wrist behind your back.

3. The hands and arms stay relaxed.

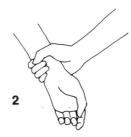

4

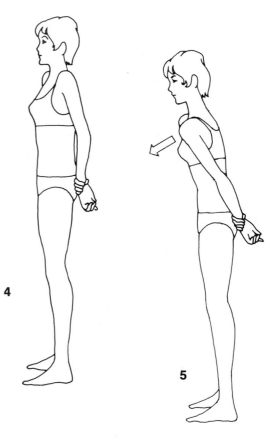

4

5

4. Starting with your shoulders relaxed in the down position, inhale, rotating them forward, up, back, down and around, making 2½ circles, ending with your shoulders in the up position. The circular motion of the shoulders is smooth.

The hands maintain contact with the lower back and do not move very much. Let your shoulders originate the movement and your arms will follow.

5. Exhale sharply, contracting your shoulders forward. Your head naturally comes slightly forward.

Do the exercise 6 times.
Do 1 *integration breath.*

ARM CIRCLES 6x

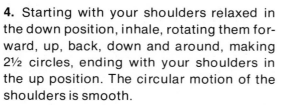

Arm circles strengthens the lungs while loosening the muscles of the shoulders, helping to free the thorax. Keeping the fingers spread stretches the muscles of the forearm.

Arm circles is a mechanical exercise which has no specific psychological effect.

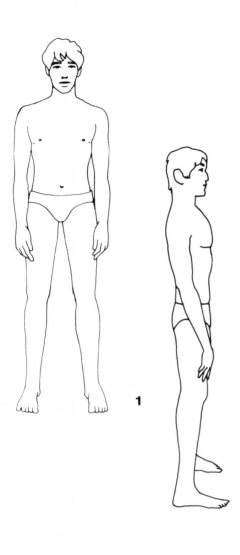

1

Procedure

Position of strength

1. Stand with your feet parallel, 3 foot-widths apart.

Your shoulders are relaxed, arms hanging at your sides.

Knees are unlocked.

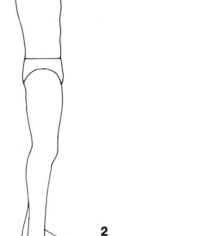

2

2. Extend your arms in front of your body at shoulder level. The palms of your hands face each other, fingers spread.

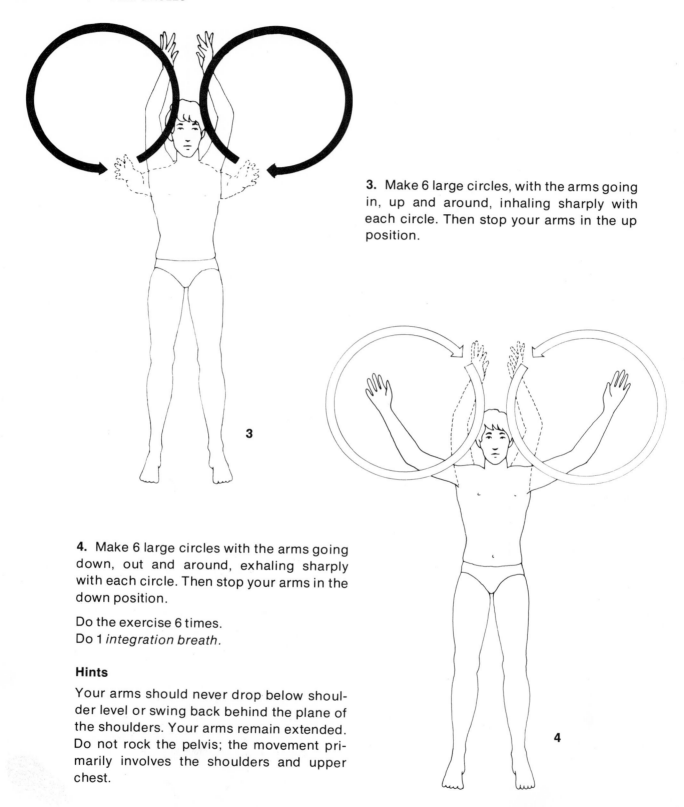

3. Make 6 large circles, with the arms going in, up and around, inhaling sharply with each circle. Then stop your arms in the up position.

3

4. Make 6 large circles with the arms going down, out and around, exhaling sharply with each circle. Then stop your arms in the down position.

Do the exercise 6 times.
Do 1 *integration breath.*

Hints

Your arms should never drop below shoulder level or swing back behind the plane of the shoulders. Your arms remain extended. Do not rock the pelvis; the movement primarily involves the shoulders and upper chest.

4

HAND CIRCLES 6x

Hand circles restores flexibility to the wrists.

Hand circles is a mechanical exercise which has no specific psychological effect.

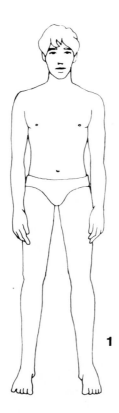

Procedure

Standing position

1. Stand with your feet parallel, 2 foot-widths apart.

Your shoulders are relaxed, arms hanging at your sides.

Knees are unlocked.

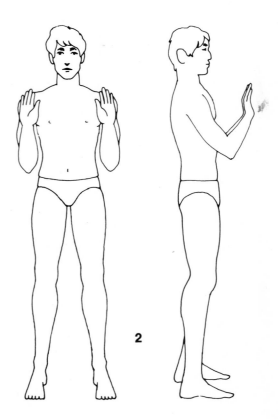

2. Raise your hands to shoulder level, palms facing forward.

Let the elbows hang relaxed. Do not clamp them to your torso. The hands remain relaxed and the movement originates in the wrists.

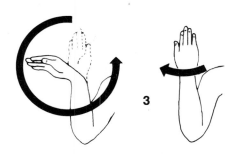

3. Rotate the wrists so that your hands move out, down and around describing a circle, ending with the palms facing the chest. Flip the hands so that the palms again face outward.

Make 6 circles, a short, sharp inhalation with each.

Flip your hands so that the palms face inward.

4. Rotate the wrists so that your hands move in, down and around describing a circle, ending with the palms facing outward. Flip the hands so that the palms face inward.

Make 6 circles, a short, sharp exhalation with each one.

Do the exercise 6 times.
Do 1 *integration breath.*

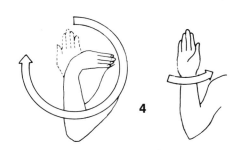

WINDMILL 3x

The *windmill* is specifically for recovering the acid-base equilibrium in the blood.

Physically, this exercise relaxes the rib cage and improves the mobility of the shoulders and hips. It also improves the metabolism.

The psychological effect is a rapid recovery from emotional stress and a return to good humor.

Procedure

Position of movement

1. Stand with your feet parallel, 1½ foot-widths apart.

Your shoulders are relaxed, arms hanging at your sides.

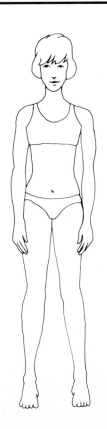

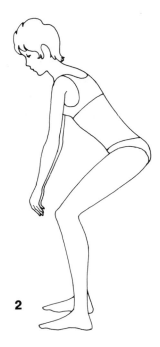

2.

2. Bend your knees and lean the torso forward. Your shoulders remain relaxed, arms loosely hanging down in front of you.

3. Inhaling evenly, make 6 backward circles, 3 with each arm, beginning with the left arm. The right arm starts its first backward circle when the left arm reaches the top of its first swing. The arms maintain this relative position throughout the backward and the forward circles.

While holding your breath, make 16 more backward circles, 8 with each arm.

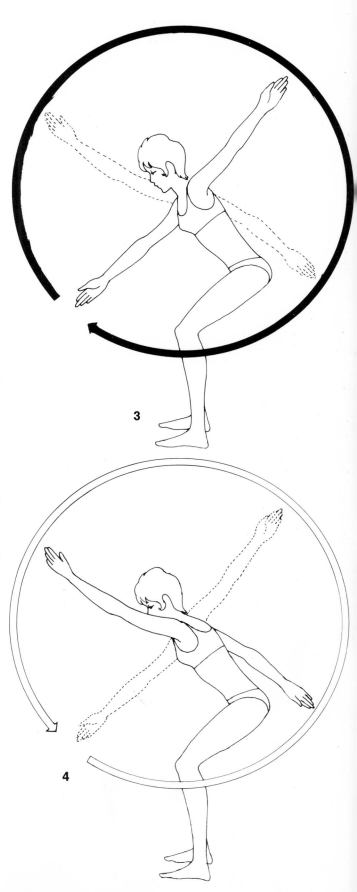

3.

4. Exhaling evenly, make 6 forward circles, 3 with each arm.

Do the exercise 3 times.
Do 1 *integration breath.*

4.

Hints

Allow the movement to originate in the knees and hips. Imagine your arms are chains which are flung into their circular orbit by momentum generated in the hips.

Check your feet: has the position changed, are they still parallel? If they have moved, you are making the arm movement too violently.

SCYTHE 6x

The *scythe* provides a vigorous twist of the spine and pelvis, stretching the internal muscles of the pelvis. This is important because it prevents the atrophy of the spinal column, a primary cause of aging. The *scythe* massages the kidneys and adrenals, increasing circulation and cleansing the blood. The urinary tract and the internal sexual organs are directly benefited.

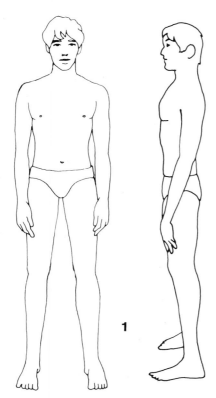

1

Procedure

Position of strength

1. Stand with your feet parallel, 3 foot-widths apart.

Your shoulders are relaxed, arms hanging at your sides.

Bend your knees.

2. Extend your arms forward at shoulder level, palms facing down.

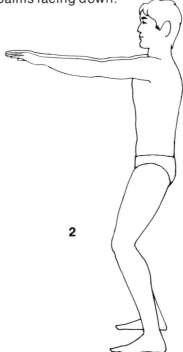

2

3. Inhale, throwing your arms to the left as far as possible. Allow the hips and torso to swing to the left with the movement. The head follows the movement of the torso.

Imagine that you are vigorously throwing something away behind you.

Extend the swing as far backward as you can to create the greatest possible stretch of the spinal column and the long muscles of the trunk. Keep the arms roughly parallel and don't let the forward arm hit against the chest. Don't let your arms drop below shoulder level.

4. Exhale, returning your arms forward to the center.

Inhale, swinging your arms to the right.

Exhale, swinging your arms forward to the center.

The movement of the *scythe* is continuous.

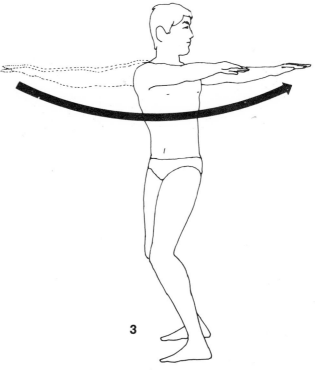

3

Do the exercise 6 times.
Do 1 *integration breath.*

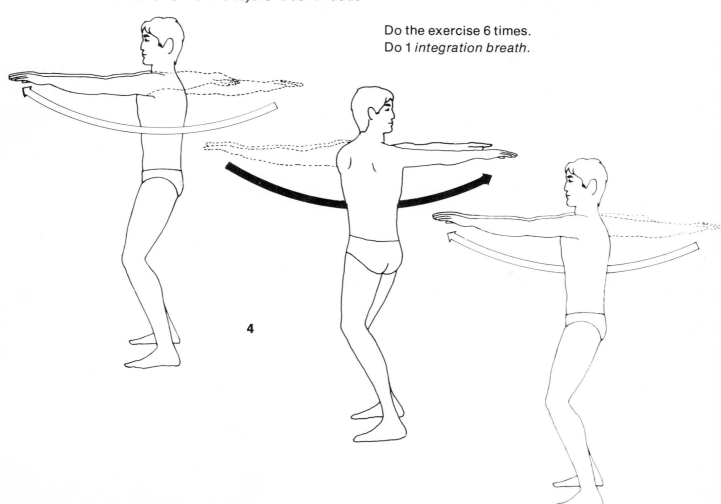

4

Neck Series

HEAD CIRCLES 6x

The *neck series* works to restore flexibility and elasticity to the muscles of the throat and neck. Any tension in this area has a direct effect on the cervical vertebrae, particularly on the top vertebra, the atlas, which supports the head. These vertebrae set the tone for the rest of the spine. If the muscles surrounding them stiffen, this is felt throughout the entire body.

Day-to-day anxieties are often felt as tension in the neck, shoulders and upper back, and these exercises deal with this tension directly.

Psychologically, the *neck series* restores the balance of the central and peripheral nervous systems.

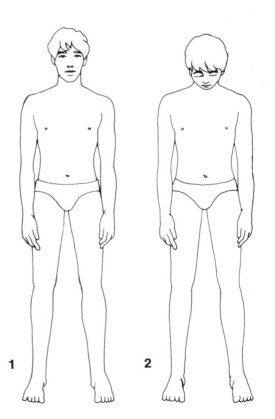

Procedure

Standing position

1. Stand with your feet parallel, 2 foot-widths apart.

Your shoulders are relaxed, arms hanging at your sides.

Knees are unlocked.

2. Let your head fall forward.

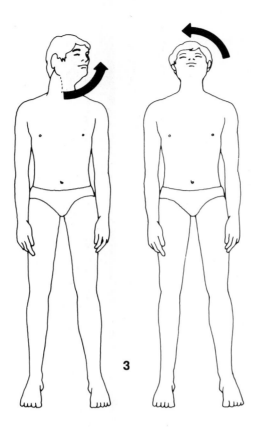

3. Inhaling, rotate your head in a half-circle toward the left, up and back.

Allow your head to roll freely, keeping your shoulders and the rest of your body relaxed.

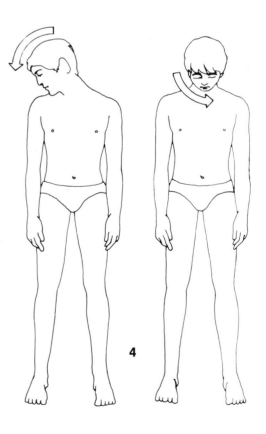

4. Exhaling, continue the circle to the right, down and forward.

The movement is continuous.

All the crackles and pops you will experience at first are due to tension.

Do 6 circles to the left, then reversing the direction, 6 circles to the right.

Neck Series

SIDE-TO-SIDE   6x

This exercise works directly to restore the separation between the head and the atlas. The spinal cord, made up of nerve pathways from and to the entire body, enters the brain through the atlas. Any constriction in this area decreases our sensitivity.

Procedure

Standing position

1. Stand with your feet parallel, 2 foot-widths apart.

Your shoulders are relaxed, arms hanging at your sides.

Knees are unlocked.

Head and neck are upright.

Your chin is tucked in.

2. Inhale, rotating your head until it faces left. Your eyes move along a horizontal plane.

Make certain that the vertebrae of the neck stay in line with the rest of the spine.

3. Exhale, rotating your head through the starting position until it faces right. The eyes maintain their movement along a horizontal plane.

The movement is continuous.

Do the exercise 6 times.

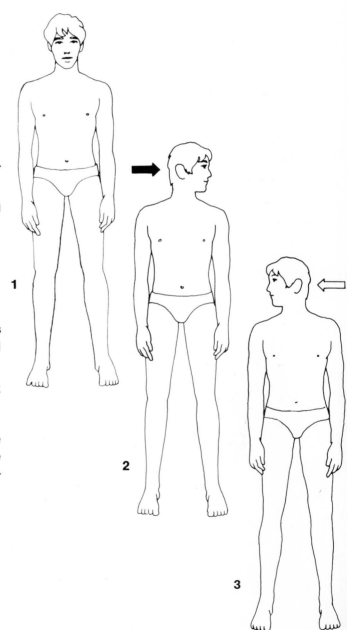

Neck Series

CAMEL 6x

The *camel* is an exercise for the throat and the muscles related to the throat.

The *camel* massages the thyroid and parathyroid glands, giving us more energy.

Procedure

Standing position

1. Stand with your feet parallel, 2 foot-widths apart.

Your shoulders are relaxed, arms hanging at your sides.

Knees are unlocked.

Pull your chin in and up.

2. Inhaling, make a half-circle with your chin, forward and down.

Confine the movement to the neck and head; the rest of the body remains relaxed.

3. Exhaling, pull your chin in and up. The movement is continuous.

Do the exercise 6 times.

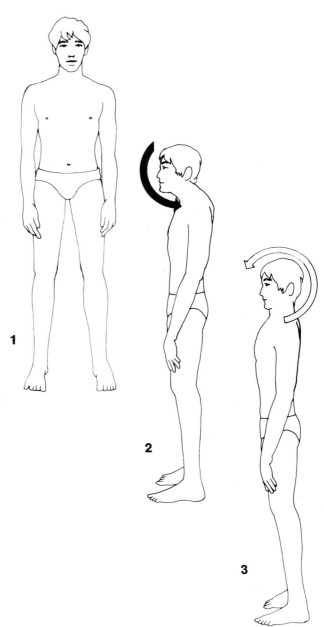

Neck Series

LUNG BREATH   6x

This is a breathing exercise for the expansion of the upper thorax.

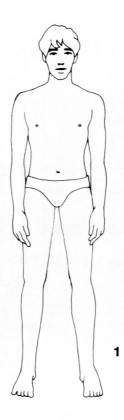

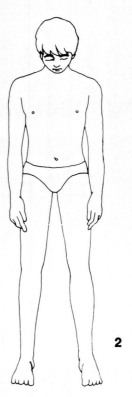

Procedure

Standing position

1. Stand with your feet parallel, 2 foot-widths apart.

Your shoulders are relaxed, arms hanging at your sides.

Knees are unlocked.

2. Let your head fall forward.

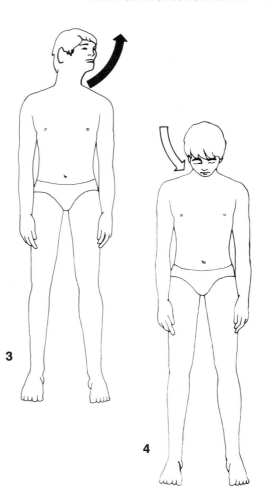

3. Inhaling, and keeping your chin close to your chest, rotate your head in an arc upward and over the left shoulder. Hold this position a moment, retaining the breath. Feel the stretch in the muscles of the right side of the neck and over the upper lobe of the right lung.

Keep the movement slow enough to fill the lungs completely, particularly the upper lobes of the lungs.

4. Exhaling, let your head rotate back down to the front.

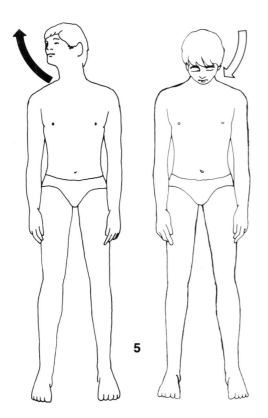

5. Repeat the movement to the right.

Confine the movements to the neck and head; the rest of the body remains relaxed.

Do the exercise 6 times.
Do 1 *integration breath.*

CANDLE 1x

The *candle* is an exercise from Hatha Yoga.

The vertical position of the *candle* uses the weight of the body to loosen and stretch the cervical vertebrae and the attachments of the skull to the top vertebra, the atlas.

Only when this connection between the atlas and the skull is flexible can the rest of the spine achieve flexibility.

The second position of the *candle*, with the balls of the feet touching the floor behind you, stretches the neck, all the back muscles, the muscles of the thighs and knees, and also the Achilles tendon.

Psychologically, the *candle* increases the sensitivity of the entire nervous system.

1

Procedure

1. Lie on your back, relax, and place your arms at your sides.

Breathe normally.

2. Raise your legs to a vertical position.

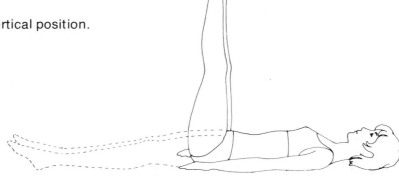

2

3. Lift your torso off the floor using your hands to support your back. Place your hands on the rib cage as close to your shoulders as possible.

The torso and legs are in a straight line, toes pointed up. The weight of the body rests on the shoulders and lower neck.

Hold this position for up to 3 minutes.

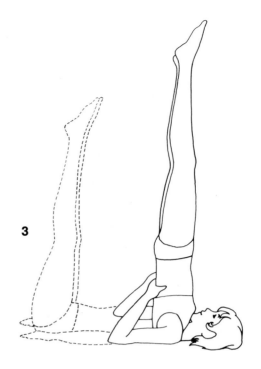

3

4

4. Keeping your knees straight, slowly and evenly lower your legs until the balls of your feet touch the floor. This stretches the Achilles tendons. Keep the upper back straight.

Relax and breathe normally.

Hold this position for up to 3 minutes.

5. Keeping your legs straight, raise them slowly and evenly to the vertical position.

Your hands support your back.

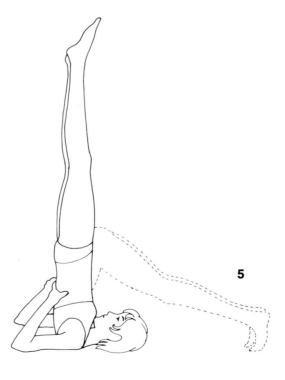

5

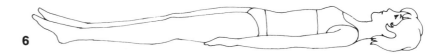

6. Lower your legs and return to the starting position.

Do the exercise once.

Hints

It may take several weeks before the *candle* comes naturally. In the meantime, work in a relaxed manner. On some days you will find this exercise easier to do than on others, or practice it later in the day when your body is looser. Do not push yourself. Lower your legs only as close to the floor behind you as you can without bending your knees.

Belly Series

BOW 6x

The *bow, leg circles* and *leg scissors* comprise the *belly series.* The *belly series* invigorates the abdominal muscles and massages the viscera: specifically the liver, gall bladder, pancreas, stomach and intestinal tract. The viscera are connected to the brain by the vagus nerve. Trouble in the viscera results in headaches, lethargy and low energy.

Psychologically, improvement in the condition of the viscera clears the mind.

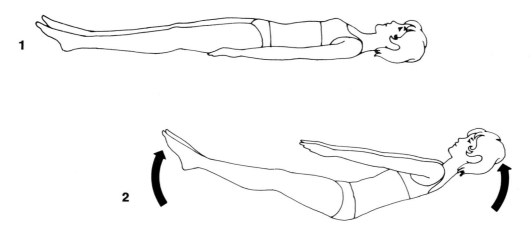

Procedure

1. Lie on your back, arms at your sides, palms down.

2. In two distinct stages, inhaling sharply with each, raise your legs and torso simultaneously, so that the weight of your body is supported by your buttocks.

3. In two distinct stages, exhaling sharply with each, allow your body to return to the starting position.

The movements are continuous and rapid.

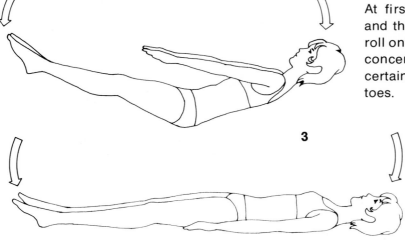

3

Don't let the breathing lag behind the movements.

Do the exercise 6 times.

Hints

At first this exercise may seem awkward and there will be a tendency to fall over or roll onto your back. This is counteracted by concentrating on the breathing and making certain that your hands point toward your toes.

Belly Series

LEG CIRCLES   6x

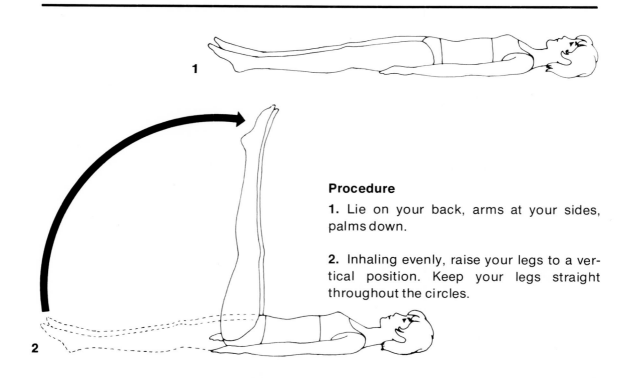

1

2

Procedure

1. Lie on your back, arms at your sides, palms down.

2. Inhaling evenly, raise your legs to a vertical position. Keep your legs straight throughout the circles.

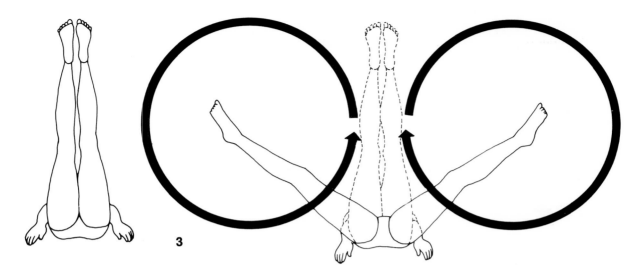

3. Continuing to inhale, make a large circle with your legs, going out, down, around and back up to the vertical position.

In the down position, your heels are 6 to 12 inches off the floor.

4. Exhaling evenly, make a large circle with your legs, coming down, out, around and back to the down position.

Keep your pelvis on the floor and make the belly muscles do the work. Don't let your hips come up and down off the floor as you make the circles.

Do the exercise 6 times.

Hints

If you find it difficult to keep your balance, place your hands under your buttocks.

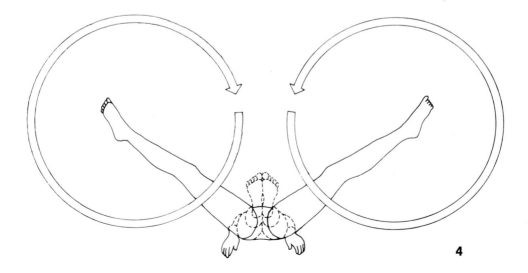

Belly Series

LEG SCISSORS 6x

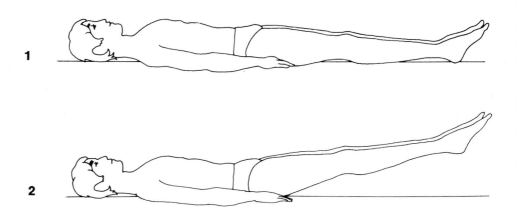

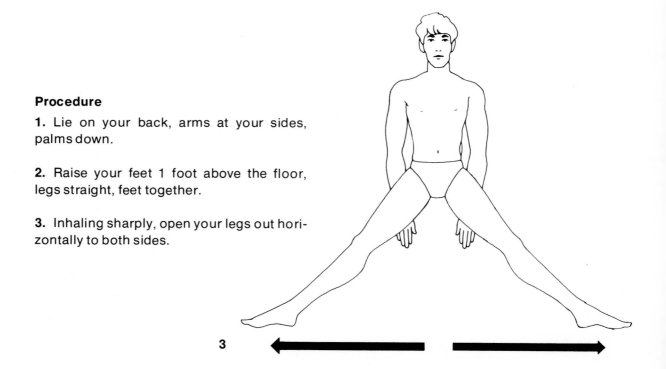

Procedure

1. Lie on your back, arms at your sides, palms down.

2. Raise your feet 1 foot above the floor, legs straight, feet together.

3. Inhaling sharply, open your legs out horizontally to both sides.

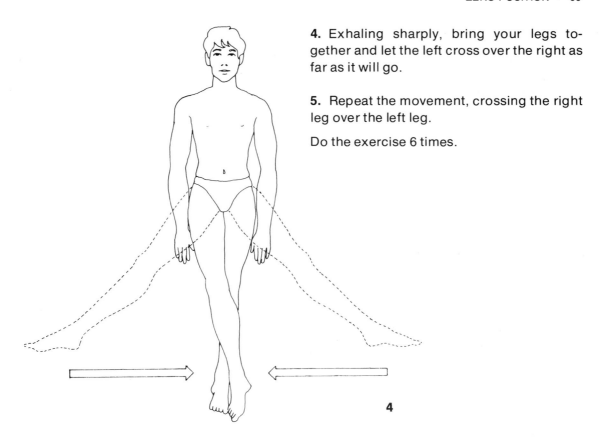

4. Exhaling sharply, bring your legs together and let the left cross over the right as far as it will go.

5. Repeat the movement, crossing the right leg over the left leg.

Do the exercise 6 times.

4

ZERO POSITION 1x

Zero position is a position for meditation. It is a precise position for relaxation and self-remembering. Within the sequence it provides a period to become conscious of our breathing and of our entire body.

Psychologically, the *zero position* is a powerful reminder that we are on the earth. We are all governed by natural laws as real as the law of gravity. In the *zero position* we become aware of the gravitational force that holds us to the earth.

Zero position is considered a sacred position. It is sacred because its effect is mystical. No one would ever choose to lie in this position of stress. It is one of the most unnatural positions that a human being can easily assume. *Zero position* forces you to remember yourself because, lying face down on the earth, there is nothing else to do. This is a totally mechanical way of reaching a serene meditative state.

In the *zero position* you give yourself up to the natural laws of reality.

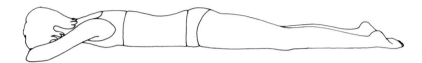

Procedure

Lie face down on the floor.

The palm of your left hand rests on the floor with the right hand covering it. Your forehead rests on the back of your right hand.

Your legs are relaxed, heels pointing out, big toes touching.

Breathe normally.

Hold this position for 1 to 3 minutes.

Do the exercise once.

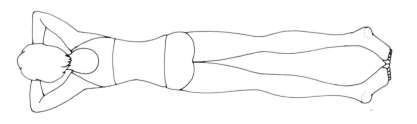

COBRA 3x

This is an exercise from Hatha Yoga.

The *cobra* uses the force of gravity to stretch the spinal column. The spine bends backward to relax the vertebrae of the lower back. The movement of the *cobra* massages the spinal column and the nerves that connect with the cerebral cortex. The *cobra* strengthens the entire nervous system.

Psychologically, the *cobra* relaxes the mind.

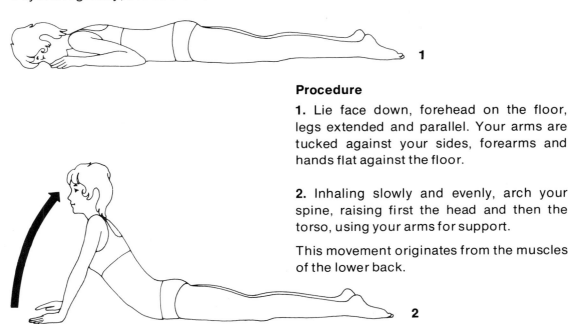

Procedure

1. Lie face down, forehead on the floor, legs extended and parallel. Your arms are tucked against your sides, forearms and hands flat against the floor.

2. Inhaling slowly and evenly, arch your spine, raising first the head and then the torso, using your arms for support.

This movement originates from the muscles of the lower back.

3. When you have risen as high as you can in this way, continue the movement by straightening your arms. Go no higher than you can without lifting your pelvis off the floor.

Your shoulders, buttocks, and the backs of your thighs and your feet are relaxed.

Hold this position while taking 3 even breaths.

4. Exhaling slowly and evenly, return to the starting position. The forehead is the last part of the body to touch the floor.

Do the exercise 3 times.
Stand up and do 1 *integration breath.*

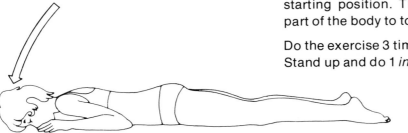

PENDULUM 20x

The *pendulum* is an exercise in balance. All the muscles of one foot and leg must work together to support the body while the other leg swings free. The entire musculature is involved in maintaining the body's equilibrium.

Our feet are among the most sensitive parts of our body. As the stationary foot adusts its position to maintain our equilibrium, the floor massages the sole of the foot. The various muscles and bones of the foot and ankle massage each other. This gradually spreads the foot, making it a broader support of our weight.

The *pendulum* strengthens the legs. Because of the coordination required to keep the entire body balanced around one simple movement, the *pendulum* develops deeper awareness of the body and of ourselves.

This exercise improves the condition of the spine and improves walking.

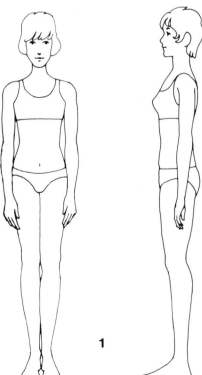

Procedure

Position of equilibrium

1. Stand with your feet together.

Your shoulders are relaxed, arms hanging at your sides.

Knees are unlocked.

Head and back are straight.

1

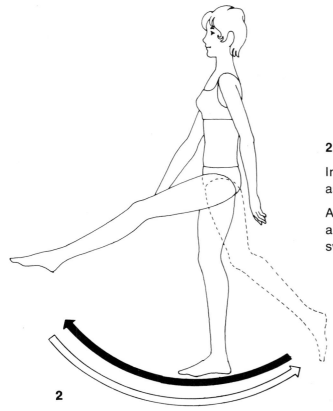

2. Place your weight on your right foot.

Inhaling, swing your left leg as far forward as possible, keeping it relaxed.

As your left leg swings forward, your right arm swings forward and your left arm swings back in a loose, relaxed motion.

3. Exhaling, swing your left leg back as far as possible, like a pendulum.

As your left leg swings back, your right arm swings back and your left arm swings forward in a loose, relaxed motion.

Fixing your eyes on a point on the wall helps maintain balance.

Swing your left leg 20 times, then your right leg 20 times.

Do 1 *integration breath.*

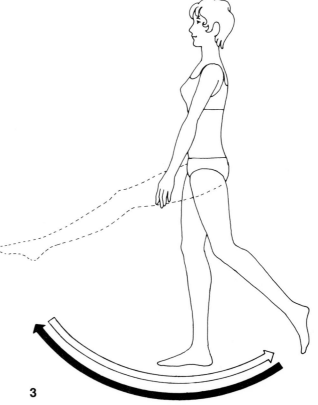

COMPLETO 3x

The *completo* is a vigorous exercise which provides a complete stretch for the whole body, made in one long breath. Like *picking grapes,* the *completo* integrates breathing and movement in which the entire skeletal structure is contracted and extended.

Physically, it increases the circulation of blood to all the organs.

Psychologically, it results in increased self-awareness.

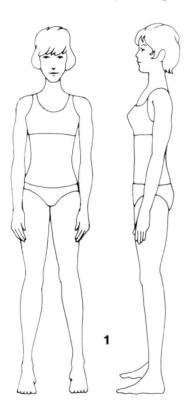

Procedure

Position of movement

1. Stand with your feet parallel, 1½ footwidths apart.

Your shoulders are relaxed, arms hanging at your sides.

Knees are relaxed.

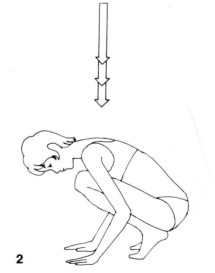

2. Exhale, letting your body drop into a crouch, palms on the floor.

Bounce 2 more times in this position, exhaling sharply with each bounce. Pump all the air out of your lungs.

3. Keeping your lungs empty, straighten your arms and step back with your left foot, then with your right foot, until your legs and back are straight. Your legs stay close together. The balls of your feet touch the floor.

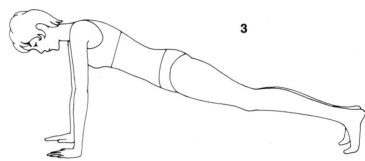

3

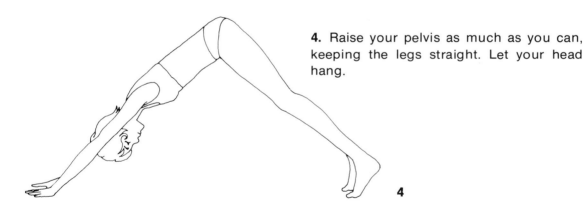

4

4. Raise your pelvis as much as you can, keeping the legs straight. Let your head hang.

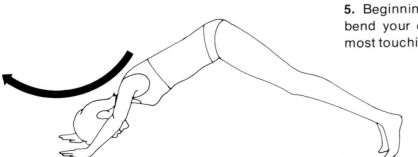

5

5. Beginning to inhale, drop your pelvis, bend your elbows and scoop forward, almost touching your nose to the floor.

6. Still inhaling, drop your pelvis close to the floor. At the same time, your elbows straighten as your head moves forward and up.

7. Still inhaling, raise your pelvis as much as you can, keeping your legs straight.

8. Still inhaling, drop your pelvis to the floor, keeping your arms straight.

9. Still inhaling, raise your pelvis again.

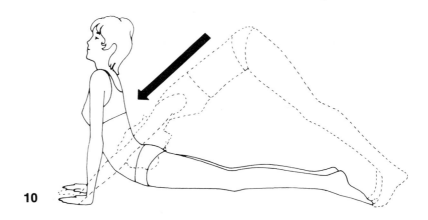

10. Still inhaling, drop your pelvis one last time.

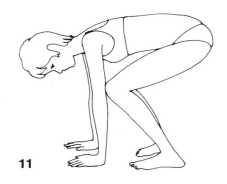

11. Holding your breath, jump forward into the crouch position. Your palms are still on the floor. Try to land with your feet 2 foot-widths apart.

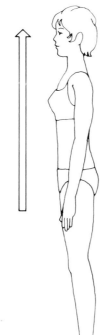

12. Exhaling, rise to a standing position, arms at your sides.

Do this exercise in one continuous movement.

Do 3 sets with an *integration breath* between each two.

Finish the sequence with 3 *integration breaths.*

Hints

Aim at making the sequence of movements fluid and smooth. Be sure to check your foot position before each *integration breath* and each *completo.* The foot positions given are those which ensure the correct sequence of movements.

part two Advanced Stages

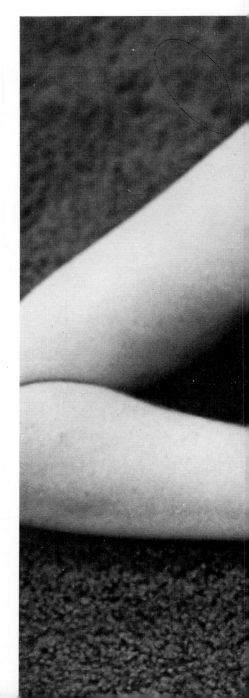

# of Psychocalisthenics

STAGE TWO | MUSCULAR CONDITIONING

When you are able to do the entire *psychocalisthenics* sequence from memory, you are ready for the second stage, which is muscular conditioning and fast movement. Increase your speed of doing the exercises approximately thirty percent. Continue spending about 30 minutes on the sequence, allowing more time for the *headstand,* the *candle,* the *zero position* and the *cobra.*

Muscular conditioning is accomplished when you can do the sequence of exercises in 30 minutes easily without pain or exhaustion. When the exercises are done this way, the muscles are put in balance; that is, one group of muscles is rebalanced in proportion to all the rest of the groups of muscles in the body. At this point the exercises become mechanical; the muscles perform the movements without fatigue. For fast movement concentrate on the movement itself, thinking that you are doing each exercise quickly and strongly. Your inhalation and exhalation must also be fast and strong. This kind of breathing opens the lungs and makes the connection between breathing and movement.

STAGE THREE | EMOTIONAL CONDITIONING

In this stage, make the movements of your body elastic as you do the exercises. The breath, not the muscles, makes the movements. The idea is to train your breath and movement to work together. When this happens the exercises become easy, and you measure the movements with the breath, not the breath by the movements. Do the exercises approximately thirty percent slower than in *stage one.*

When the movements are controlled by the breath, they become internalized, that is, conscious. External movement, which is controlled by the large muscles, is fast, so fast that we lose the consciousness of it. Internal movement is slow and allows us to feel the movement consciously.

When we allow our breath to make the movements, our lungs are fully ventilated and our emotional balance improves. Our emotional states depend upon the acid-base equilibrium of our blood. If our blood is too acidic, the result is depression or bad humor. If our blood is too alkaline, the result is overenthusiasm which causes us to burn more energy than is needed for any given activity. The regulation of the acid-base balance in our blood with the breathing exercises of *psychocalisthenics* governs our emotional balance and controls the body.

STAGE FOUR | KINESTHETIC MOVEMENT

To refine our sense of the movements, we need to make them even slower. When a movement is fast, we lose consciousness of it as a movement occurring within our body. To feel consciously, we have to move consciously in slow motion. This gives us the kinesthetic impression of our body. Then we become aware of the kinesthetic relation of our bones and muscles and our whole body as a totality. With kinesthetic movement we feel the joints changing their position. Then we are truly aware of the movement of our body from the inside, or conscious, point of view. We are aware of what we are doing rather than of how we are doing it. The breathing governs the movements.

Regulation of the breathing is accomplished by using the counting system. Each exercise is broken down into distinct units, each of which requires a given number of beats. The beats are of equal length throughout the sequence. At first, the length of the beat depends on how fast you can do the exercise and still retain a kinesthetic awareness of it. Eventually the rhythm can be that of your heartbeat.

In this stage we make the link of our kinesthetic sensibility, which makes the unity of the three elements: mind, body and emotions. We have the counting for the mind, the inhaling of the breath for the emotions and the slow motion for the physical body. When we have finished this stage, we will find that the mechanical repetition of the counting has created an internal rhythm, with a kind of internal melody that comes with that rhythm.

If you wish to go on to advanced kinesthetic movement, refer to the special kinesthetic sequence in Psychocalisthenics Exercises for Special Purposes.

In *stage five, psychocalisthenics* becomes a meditation in movement.

Integration breath

Standing position/2 foot-widths
- Count 6 beats from the start to the top of the movement.
- Count 3 beats from the top to the end of the movement.
- Count 6 beats as the arms move down with the exhalation.
- Count 3 beats as the movement finishes.
- The movement and breathing are continuous and never broken.
- Do three 6–3–6–3 *integration breaths* at the beginning and end of *stage four psychocalisthenics.*

Do one 6–3–6–3 *integration breath* wherever an *integration breath* is indicated in earlier levels.

Headstand

- After going up into the position, breathe through the nose in the following pattern:

    3 breaths: 3 beats inhaling, 3 beats exhaling

    3 breaths: 6 beats inhaling, 6 beats exhaling
- Repeat this pattern for the duration of the exercise.

Picking grapes

Standing position/2 foot-widths
- Exhale in 1 beat.
- Inhale in 8 beats, 1 beat for each pump and 1 beat for each stretch.
- Repeat 6 times.

Lateral stretch

Position of strength/3 foot-widths
- 1 beat on the inhale, stretching to the side.
- 1 beat on the exhale, dropping into the crouch position.
- Repeat 6 times.

Flamingo

Position of movement/1½ foot-widths
- 6 beats down on inhalation.
- 3 beats transition at the end of the movement.
- 6 beats up on the exhalation.
- 3 beats transition at the end of the movement.
- Repeat 6 times.
- The breath is never held; it slows and reverses direction.

Ax 1

Position of relaxation/5 foot-widths
- 3 beats inhaling to the top of the arc, 3 beats exhaling to the bottom of the arc.
- Reverse direction, repeat 6 times.

With the kinesthetic movement here, there is no pendulum effect as in *ax 1* in the previous stages.

Ax 2

Position of relaxation/5 foot-widths
- 3 complete circles inhaling, 1 beat per circle.
- At the end of the third circle, exhale in a burst.
- Reverse direction.
- Repeat 3 times.

Udiyama

Position of strength/3 foot-widths
This exercise is practiced as in the earlier levels.

Shoulder rolls

Standing position/2 foot-widths
- 6 circles inhaling, 1 beat per circle.
- Expel breath sharply.
- Repeat 6 times.

Arm circles

Position of strength/3 foot-widths
- 6 circles inhaling, 1 beat per circle.
- 6 circles exhaling, 1 beat per circle.
- Repeat 6 times.

Hand circles

Standing position/2 foot-widths
- 6 circles inhaling, 1 beat per circle.
- 6 circles exhaling, 1 beat per circle.
- Repeat 6 times.

Windmill

Position of movement/1½ foot-widths
- 6 beats with backward movement, inhaling.
- 16 beats with backward movement, holding breath.
- 6 beats with forward movement, exhaling.
- Repeat 6 times.

Scythe

Position of strength/3 foot-widths
- 1 beat to left, inhaling.
- 1 beat to center, exhaling.
- 1 beat to right, inhaling.
- 1 beat to center, exhaling.
- Repeat 6 times.
- The movement must be relaxed like a dance.

Neck series
Head circles

Standing position/2 foot-widths
- 3 beats to top, inhaling.
- 3 beats to bottom, exhaling.
- Repeat 6 times to the left, then 6 times to the right.

Neck series
Side-to-side

Standing position/2 foot-widths
- 1 beat to left, inhaling.
- 1 beat to right, exhaling.
- Repeat 6 times.

Neck series
Camel

Standing position/2 foot-widths
- 3 beats inhaling.
- 3 beats exhaling.
- Repeat 6 times.

Neck series
Lung breath
Standing position/2 foot-widths
- 3 beats with upward motion, inhaling.
- 3 beats with breath held.
- 3 beats with downward motion, exhaling.
- There is no retention of breath at the bottom of the cycle.
- Repeat 6 times.

Candle
- In the vertical position of the *candle,* breathe in the following pattern:
    3 breaths: 3 beats inhaling, 3 beats exhaling
    3 breaths: 6 beats inhaling, 6 beats exhaling
- In the other steps the breathing is free.

Belly series
Bow
- 1 beat to knee level, inhaling.
- 1 beat the rest of the way up, inhaling.
- 1 beat down to knee level, exhaling.
- 1 beat down to floor level, exhaling.
- Repeat 6 times.

Belly series
Leg circles
- 3 beats inhaling.
- 3 beats exhaling.
- Repeat 6 times.

Belly series
Leg scissors
- 1 beat inhaling.
- 1 beat exhaling.
- Repeat 6 times.

Zero position
This exercise is practiced as in earlier levels.

Cobra
- Stay up for 3 beats, holding breath.
- Repeat 3 times.

Pendulum
Position of equilibrium/feet together
- 1 beat kicking forward, inhaling.
- 1 beat kicking back, exhaling.
- Repeat 20 times on each leg.

Completo
Position of movement/1½ foot-widths
- 3 beats exhaling, 1 for each bounce.
- 3 beats holding breath:
    1 beat as left foot goes back
    1 beat as right foot goes back
    1 beat raising the pelvis
- 6 beats inhaling on the dips:
    2 beats scooping forward
    1 beat raising the pelvis
    1 beat lowering the pelvis
    1 beat raising the pelvis
    1 beat lowering the pelvis
- 3 beats exhaling:
    1 beat jumping forward
    1 beat standing up
    1 beat bringing hands together for *integration breath.*
- Change foot position to *standing position.*

STAGE FIVE |
BREATHING THE 9 COLORS

In *stage five* of *psychocalisthenics* we breathe the nine colors. Do this by imagining that the air you inhale is the color. On the inhalation, feel your lungs fill with air and color, and on the exhalation, feel the color spread throughout your whole body. Each of the nine colors you inhale corresponds to one aspect of consciousness. Do one color each day by following the sequence of the nine colors of the spectrum in this order: dark blue, light blue, dark green, light green, yellow, orange, red, violet-red and violet. This stage, though simple, is the highest and most complete of *psychocalisthenics,* provided that all of the previous stages have been mastered. With mastery of the other stages, this stage is a complete meditation. Meditation here means to concentrate your mind in your physical body. The input of your consciousness is inside of your body. This links the two parts of your consciousness, mind and body, making a unity.

Continue using the counting system of *stage four.*

part three

Psychocalisthenics

Exercises
for
Special Purposes

STRESS SITUATIONS

Windmill	3 times
Flamingo	1 time
Zero position	1 time
Integration breath	9 times

The key exercise for combating unusual stress is the *windmill.* For situations where you are nervous or excited the *zero position* is recommended.

QUICK ENERGY

Picking grapes	12 times
Integration breath	3 times

DESKBOUND SEQUENCE

Shoulder rolls	6 times (seated)
Integration breath	3 times (seated)
Neck series	
Head circles	6 times (seated)
Side-to-side	6 times (seated)
Camel	6 times (seated)
Lung breath	6 times (seated)
Hand circles	6 times (seated)

If space permits, add the *completo,* a classic exercise for limbering up after you have been seated for hours. Also recommended are the *lateral stretch* and the *pendulum.* Do these exercises at a slower tempo than usual.

MORNING-AFTER EXERCISE

Procedure

Standing position

1. Stand with feet parallel, 2 foot-widths apart. The shoulders are relaxed, arms hanging at the sides. Join the hands, fingers loosely interlaced. Relax the arms, letting them hang in front of the body. Bend over as far as possible and hold this position until you feel pressure in the head.

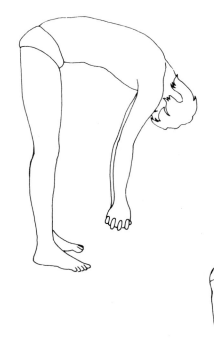

1

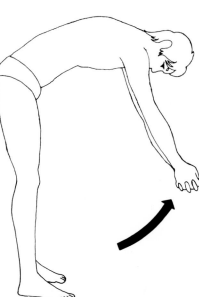

2. Inhaling evenly, straighten up. As you do so, let your extended arms float up.

2

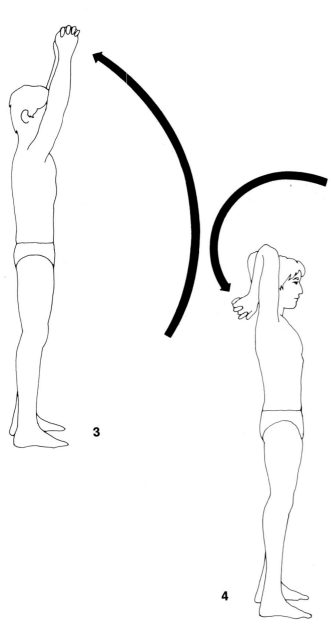

3. Continuing to inhale evenly, slowly raise the arms up over the head.

4. Slow the inhalation as the hands and forearms continue the movement. When the clasped hands are behind the back of the neck, press them lightly together.

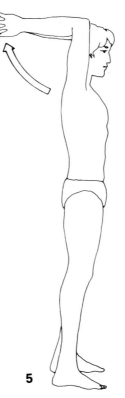

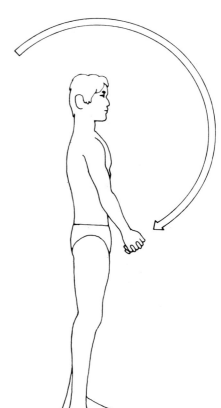

5. Exhaling evenly, slowly bring hands and forearms over the head.

6. Continue the exhalation and, keeping your arms extended, return to the standing position.

Repeat 12 times from step 2.

QUICK PSYCHOCALISTHENICS

For occasions when sufficient time is not available for the full sequence.

1. Exercises normally repeated 6 times, repeat 3 times.
2. Exercises normally repeated 3 times, do once (except for 3 *integration breaths* at the beginning and end of the sequence).
3. Where 1–3 minutes is indicated, do 1 minute.
4. In the *pendulum,* do 10 swings per leg.

RECUPERATION PSYCHOCALISTHENICS

Check with your doctor about the advisability of doing any exercise you feel might be a strain. Reduce the number of repetitions as in *quick psychocalisthenics,* and also reduce the tempo.

PHYSICAL CONDITIONING

For endurance, speed and precision of movement, the following sequence is recommended:

1. Double the repetitions from 6 to 12, from 3 to 6.
2. Where 1 of an exercise is indicated, repeat 3 times.
3. Hold *headstand* and *candle* for 3 to 6 minutes.
4. Cautiously increase the amount of time spent in the *cobra.*

At first this sequence will take an hour. The ideal time is 40 to 45 minutes.

SPECIAL KINESTHETIC SEQUENCE

This sequence has been designed to deepen the experience of kinesthesia. The following patterns of breathing and movement are substituted for those in *stage four.* With these more advanced patterns the sequence can take several hours to complete. It is possible, however, to work through the series over a number of sessions, experiencing different exercises as independent meditations in movement.

Integration breath

- 3 breaths with 6–3–6–3 pattern.
- 3 breaths with 12–6–12–6 pattern.
- Use this pattern at the beginning and end of the sequence. Between exercises, use the 6–3–6–3 pattern, one time.

Headstand

- After going up into the position breathe through the nose in the following pattern:
- 3 breaths: 3 beats inhaling,   3 beats exhaling,
  3 breaths: 6 beats inhaling,   6 beats exhaling,
  3 breaths: 12 beats inhaling, 12 beats exhaling,
  3 breaths: 24 beats inhaling, 24 beats exhaling.
- Gradually work your way up through this sequence. The capacity of your lungs develops naturally.

Picking grapes

(Same as *stage four*)

Lateral stretch

(Same as *stage four*)

Flamingo

- Do the exercise 3 times using 6–3–6–3 pattern.
- Repeat 3 times using 12–6–12–6 pattern.

Ax 1

- Do the exercise 3 times using 3–3 pattern.
- Repeat 3 times with 6 beats on each inhalation and 6 beats on each exhalation.

Ax 2

(Same as *stage four*)

Udiyama

(No counting)

Shoulder rolls

(Same as *stage four*)

Arm circles

- 1 beat per circle, 6 circles inhaling.
- 1 beat per circle, 6 circles exhaling.
- Repeat 3 times.
- 1 beat per circle, 12 circles inhaling.
- 1 beat per circle, 12 circles exhaling.
- Repeat 3 times.

Hand circles

- Use same pattern as *arm circles.*

Windmill

- Do the exercise 3 times using 6–16–6 pattern.
- Do the exercise 3 times using 12–32–12 pattern. This is the absolute maximum limit on the breathing for this exercise. If carried any further it may strain the heart.

Scythe

(Same as *stage four*)

Neck series

- *Head circles, side-to-side* and *camel* are the same as *stage four.* Do the *lung breath* as follows:
- 3 times with 3–3–3 pattern.
- 3 times with 6–6–6 pattern.

Candle

- In the vertical position begin breathing through the nose in the following pattern:
- 3 breaths: 3 beats inhaling, 3 beats exhaling,
  3 breaths: 6 beats inhaling, 6 beats exhaling,
  3 breaths: 12 beats inhaling, 12 beats exhaling.
- In the other steps the breathing is free.

Belly series

(Same as *stage four*)

Zero position

(No counting)

Cobra

- Do the exercise 3 times, staying up for a count of 3 beats with the breath held.
- Do the exercise 3 times, staying up for a count of 6 beats with the breath held.

Pendulum

(Same as *stage four*)

Completo

(Same as *stage four*)

SPINAL PSYCHOCALISTHENICS

These are special exercises for relaxing and strengthening the spinal column. The entire nervous system benefits from relaxation of tensions in the spine. The sequence should be done with delicacy and a deep respect for the body. Attention is in the breathing, in the *kath point,* in the spine as a unit and in each of the vertebrae.

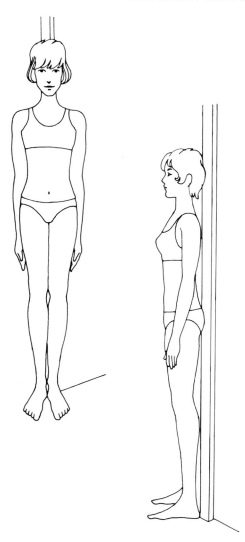

Straight spine

Procedure

Place the heels together against an outside corner. The shoulders are relaxed, arms hanging at the sides. The feet make a 45-degree angle. Heels, sacrum and the vertebrae between the shoulder blades and the back of the head touch the corner. Breathe normally. Hold this position for 1–3 minutes.

Side bend

Procedure

1. The initial position is the same as for *straight spine.*

2. Exhaling, let the upper torso follow the head in a slow bend to the left. The heels and sacrum maintain contact with the corner.

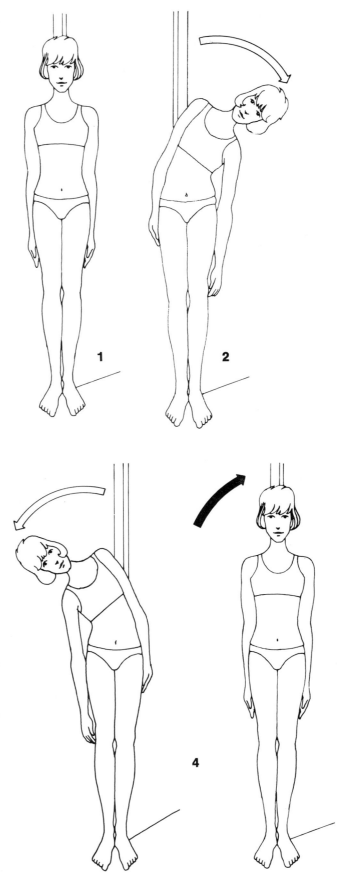

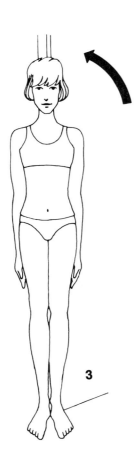

3. Inhaling, straighten to the initial position.

4. Repeat steps 2 and 3, bending to the right.

Repeat 3 times to each side.

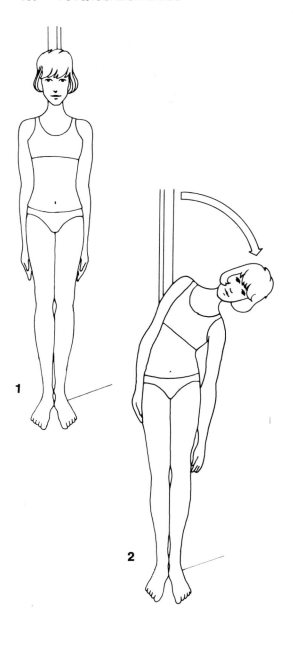

Side bend with twist

Procedure

1. The initial position is the same as for *straight spine.*

2. Exhaling, let the upper torso follow the head in a slow bend to the left. The heels and sacrum maintain contact with the corner.

3. Inhaling, reach around the corner with the top of the head.

4. Exhaling, return to step 2 position.

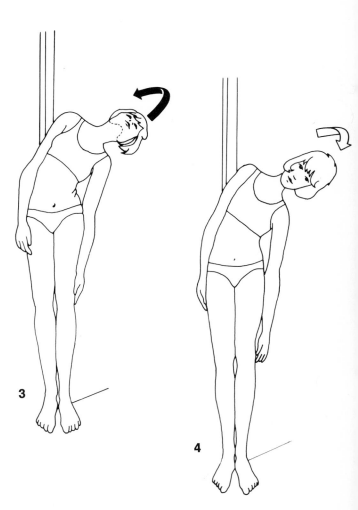

5. Inhaling, straighten to the initial position.

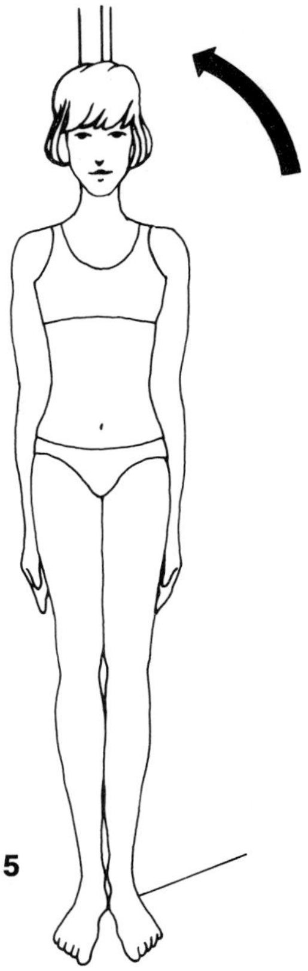

6. Repeat steps 2 through 5 to the right.

Repeat 3 times to each side.

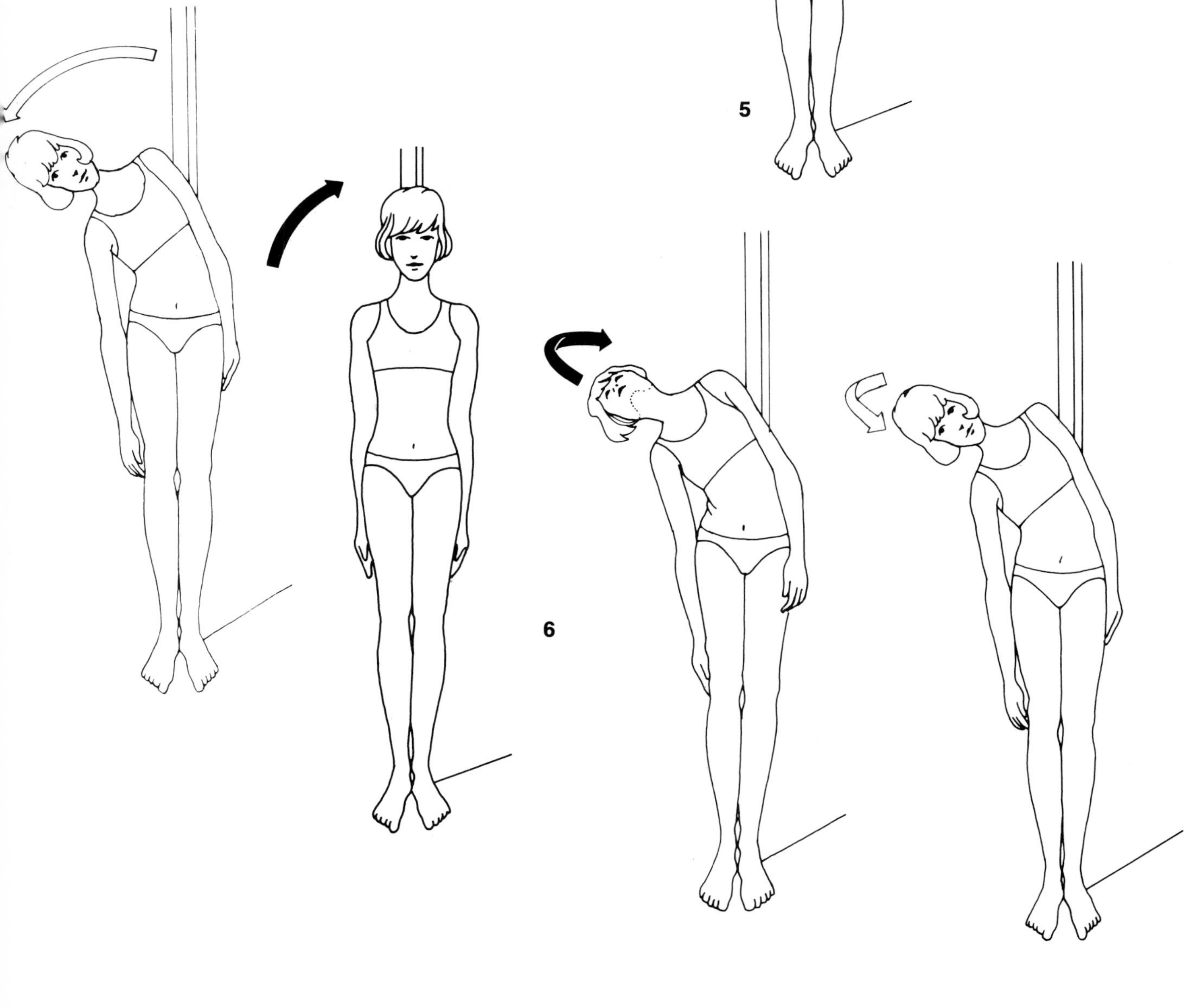

5

6

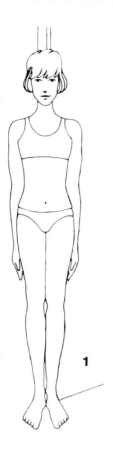

Arch

Procedure

1. The initial position is the same as for *straight spine.*

2. Reach up and grasp the corner above your head.

3. Arch your body away from the corner, keeping your heels on the floor and allowing your head to tilt back. Breathing normally, hold this position for 1 minute.

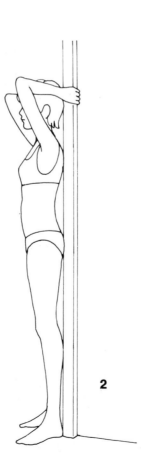

Ladder

Procedure

1. Stand with your back to the corner, about 1½ feet away.

2. Reaching up and behind you, grasp the corner above your head.

3. Breathing normally, slowly walk down the corner with your hands as you arch your back.

4. Walk back up the corner.

Repeat 3 times.

3

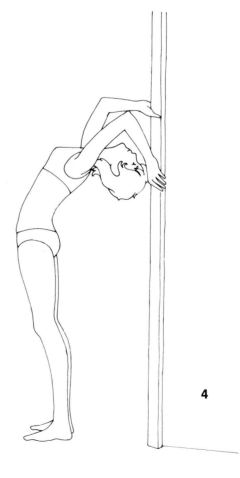

4

PSYCHOCALISTHENICS DURING PREGNANCY

Certain exercises are uncomfortable during pregnancy. The following sequence is recommended:

Integration breath
Picking grapes
Flamingo
Ax 1 and 2
Shoulder rolls
Arm circles
Hand circles
Windmill
Scythe
Neck series
   Head circles
   Side-to-side
   Camel
   Lung breath
Candle
Zero position
Cobra
Pendulum

Work with delicacy. It is possible to return to the complete sequence a week after childbirth. If you feel uncertain as to whether you should do any of the exercises, consult your doctor.

THE ARICA SYSTEM

Psychocalisthenics is one of a series of programs offered by the Arica Institute as a part of a complete Theory and System for the realization of human beings. This System is comprehensive and includes programs that develop the body and all the aspects of a human being. The System includes the nine steps of the entire human process. The Theory is the explanation of the *Unity* by the discovery of a new logic that describes *the process and the Unity of the Whole.* This has been delineated by Oscar Ichazo in a book, *The Human Process for Enlightenment and Freedom.*

Arica Institute was founded by Oscar Ichazo in 1971 in New York City for the purpose of building a mystical school to disseminate the Arica Theory and System. The Arica System, including *psychocalisthenics,* is available in book form and is also offered as Arica programs.

Psychocalisthenics is used in Arica to support the intensive process of the development of consciousness. The exercises may be learned independently for improved physical and psychic health or in conjunction with Arica Trainings.